FORMATION

The Legal and Operational Guide to Forming Your Venture Funded Company

Dr. Michael Fischer

*To the entrepreneurs brave enough to
make their dreams come true.*

Even the gods have their own laws.

— OVID, 43 BC-17 AD, ROMAN POET

CONTENTS

PREFACE

Starting a company can be a daunting task, especially if you're not familiar with the business and legal side of things. But the truth is, these are skills that anyone can learn and master. And with the guidance and roadmap provided in this book, you'll have the knowledge and confidence you need to successfully launch and grow your own company. While you certainly will need to hire people to help you, there is no substitute for knowing the material yourself.

That's why I decided to write this book. As a first-time entrepreneur, I wish I had a comprehensive guide and roadmap to help me understand the major parts of starting a company before diving in headfirst. Whether you're a technical person like me or just starting out in the business world, this book will provide you with the tools and knowledge you need to confidently and successfully launch your own company.

FORMATION

INTRODUCTION

Main points:

1. This book covers a wide range of legal and operational topics related to forming a company.
2. While the book aims to provide a comprehensive guide and roadmap, it does not cover the process of idea formation or raising money.
3. This book is not intended to be legal advice and readers should not rely on it as a substitute for seeking professional legal counsel.

Your VC said yes to investing!

...Now what?

For many entrepreneurs, securing venture funding is the point where your business becomes real—or at least it feels like it does. Your business adventure is no longer just you and a brilliant idea. Now it's you, a brilliant idea, and money.

Without a guide, forming your company can dampen your spirits, delay the launch of your product, frustrate partners, and cost you a lot of money.

This book is here to help. I'll walk you through the legal and operational steps you need to take to get from getting a verbal yes from a VC to hiring your first employee.

This book is a product of the lessons your fellow entrepreneurs have learned about the process of forming companies. I hope it will save you from sleepless nights and wasted money.

Just a note before I get started:

Disclaimer: While I did the research, this book doesn't absolve you from the responsibility of doing your own. Every entrepreneur's journey is unique, so it's a good idea to get the opinions of experts. My goal was to give you a guide and a roadmap when forming your company so that you can have a better understanding of what the process is like and so you have more background when talking with your lawyer. There will be steps in your personal journey when forming a company that are not covered in this book. I am not a lawyer, I am not your lawyer, and this book is not legal advice. Don't hold me responsible for any messy situations you get yourself in based on this book. This book does not constitute legal advice and may not reflect current laws or circumstances. The publisher and the author are providing this book and its contents on an "as is" basis. Your use of the information in this book is at your own risk.

Ok, ready to begin?

FUNDRAISING

Main points:

1. Consider whether venture fundraising is the best way to achieve your business goals.
2. Time your fundraising efforts to maximize your chances of success.
3. Plan for a 3-6 month process of building relationships with investors and raising enough money to give your company an 18-month runway.

While Venture Capital (VC) funding can greatly accelerate your business growth, it is not a fit for every company. Most businesses—particularly those with low entry costs—are more profitable (and way less risky) when they are bootstrapped. Many businesses can be funded with loans from a bank, grants from organizations, or Small Business Administration (SBA) loans from the government. Before you proceed, make sure that venture fundraising is in fact the best way to reach your business goals.

Venture fundraising could be necessary if building a thriving business in your industry requires any of the following:

1. Speed of execution (that you can't achieve by bootstrapping).
2. Credibility you don't have (but will thanks to a VC).
3. Critical mass (such as a particular share of the market).
4. High innovation costs (months or years of development, R&D, etc.).
5. Connections (the right VC could get you deals you can't on your own).

6. High entry costs (such as equipment, marketing, and so on).

If you've got an early-stage VC who wants to give you all the money you need, then congratulations! You can skip this chapter and move on to the term sheet.

Step 1: Time Your Fundraising

This step isn't a legal requirement—just a word of advice.

While there's much speculation about the perfect time to fundraise, one thing is sure: Close your deals before thanksgiving. Like the weather, VCs tend to cool off significantly during the holiday season.

Fundraising can take anywhere from a day to a few months. To be safe, plan for the fundraising process to take you months from start to finish. Closing in particular can take several weeks. With this in mind, either close in early November or wait until after the new year to launch your fundraising campaign. August is also a popular vacation month among VCs, so while some entrepreneurs say spring is an ideal fundraising time, make sure you start early enough to close before summer bogs you down.

Whatever season you choose, remember that building momentum is a key part of the fundraising process. If there are long gaps in your campaign, it will be harder to hold people's attention and build up the necessary momentum.

A general rule of thumb is to allow 3-6 months from your initial contact with an investor to getting funds in the bank. Not all this time is not spent pushing for cash, either. Much of it is spent developing a relationship with the VC. In this sense, raising capital is like dating: it doesn't work well when you're desperate. Start by reaching out to get to know the investor and make sure your first interaction with them isn't to ask for money. Also sometimes a VC will say no on one round but yes on another round, so keep them in the loop, they might be interested later.

When you do ask for money, make sure you raise enough to give your company an 18-month runway. It's not a good idea to put yourself in a place where you need to start a new fundraising round as soon as you've completed the first.

To determine very approximately how much money you should raise in your first fundraising round, map out your expected operational costs per month and multiply that by 18. Then add incorporation and fundraising costs. Then give yourself a ~50% buffer on top of that for unforeseen costs.

TERM SHEET

Main points:

1. A term sheet is a document outlining the key terms and conditions of a venture capital investment, serving as the starting point for negotiations between the entrepreneur and investor.
2. It is crucial for entrepreneurs to thoroughly review and understand the contents of a term sheet, including company valuation, investment terms, security, voting rights, liquidation preference, investor commitment, and other key elements.
3. Every part of the term sheet is negotiable, and it may be advisable to seek legal guidance to help negotiate a favorable deal.

A term sheet is a document that outlines the key terms and conditions of a venture capital investment. It serves as a starting point for negotiations between the entrepreneur and the investor, and is typically the first step in the process of closing a funding deal. Understanding the contents of a term sheet is crucial for any entrepreneur seeking venture capital funding, as it helps make informed decisions and protect their interests.

In this chapter, we will explore the key elements of a term sheet and how to interpret them. We will also discuss the role of a lawyer in the term sheet process and provide tips on how to negotiate a favorable deal. By the end of this chapter, you will have a solid understanding of what to look for in a term sheet and how to evaluate the terms being offered.

Step 2: Thoroughly Review The Term Sheet

If you haven't already, one of the first things you'll get after getting a verbal yes from a VC is a term sheet. A VC might give you a nonbinding term sheet first that explains the terms of their deal to you. This is so the VC and you can figure out the big parts of the deal before paying a lawyer to formalize it.

You should read over and understand all parts of the term sheet. Term sheets have no set formula, but they might cover the following points:

1. Company valuation: This is an estimate of the total value of the company, and is typically based on the company's potential future earnings and growth prospects. The valuation will affect how much equity the investor receives in exchange for their investment.
2. Investment terms: This section outlines the amount of money being invested and the percentage of ownership or equity that the investor will receive in return. It may also specify any restrictions on the transfer or sale of these shares.
3. Security: This section specifies the type of security the investor will receive, such as preferred stock or common stock. It may also outline the terms and conditions of these securities, such as voting rights and dividend payments.
4. Voting rights: what voting rights (and seats on the board, if applicable) investors will have.
5. Liquidation preference: This section specifies how the proceeds from a sale or liquidation of the company will be distributed among the investors, founders, and other shareholders.
6. Investor commitment: how long the investor is required to remain vested.

7. Related entity conditions (investor rights to related ventures).
8. Closing conditions (accounting and legal due diligence, how much of the fees are paid by the company, etc.).
9. Timing to close: the amount of time both parties have to come to a binding decision.
10. Any additional rights you or your VC deem important.

You will likely need to look up several phrases on the term sheet to make sure your understanding is solid. This is normal. To help you along, here are some explanations of some of the terms you're likely to run into. Every part of the term sheet is negotiable. Figure out which are important to the investor and to you, and negotiate on terms you find important.

Valuation: Valuation is an estimate of total equity (for the company as a whole). In other words, it is an estimate of what the company is worth (for brand new companies, this is a discounted reflection of what the company is estimated to be worth in the future). Note that the valuation will change once your company is funded. The value of your company before its latest round of fundraising is referred to as the "pre-money valuation." Estimating your company's value after the current round of fundraising is complete will give you the "post-money valuation." Keeping the two numbers straight is important because future investors should pay a higher price for stock (based on the valuation) since they are buying into a company with more assets.

Preferred stock, common stock, and deferred stock are all types of securities that represent ownership in a company. They differ in the rights and privileges that they offer to their holders.

Preferred stock is a type of stock that typically has a higher claim on a company's assets and earnings than common stock. Preferred shareholders are typically entitled to receive dividends before common shareholders, and they may also have the right to receive their dividends in the form of additional shares of preferred stock rather than cash. Preferred shareholders may also have the right to convert their preferred stock into common stock at a predetermined conversion ratio.

Common stock is the most widely-held type of stock and represents ownership in a company. Common shareholders have the right to vote at shareholder meetings and to receive dividends, if and when they are declared by the company's board of directors. However, common shareholders do not have any priority over preferred shareholders when it comes to receiving dividends or the company's assets in the event of a liquidation.

Deferred stock is a type of stock that does not have any voting rights or entitlement to dividends until certain conditions are met. Deferred stock may be issued to employees as part of a compensation package, and the conditions for vesting (i.e., the conditions under which the stock becomes eligible for dividends and voting rights) may be based on the employee's length of service or the achievement of certain performance milestones. Deferred stock may also be issued to investors as a way to delay the issuance of common or preferred stock until certain conditions are met. These shares are "deferred" in the sense that they will not vest until a specified date in the future. For this reason, they can be useful incentives for keeping the startup team together until the company has been a success.

Preferred stock typically has limited or no voting rights, while common stock typically has full voting rights. This means that common shareholders have the right to vote on matters related to the company, such as the election of the board of directors, changes to the company's bylaws, and major corporate actions such as mergers and acquisitions.

Preferred shareholders, on the other hand, may not have the right to vote on these matters or may only have limited voting rights. Instead, they may have certain contractual rights and preferences, such as the right to receive dividends or the right to receive a certain amount upon the liquidation or sale of the company.

Liquidation preference: This clause explains who gets paid first in a liquidity or dissolution event (if the company gets sold). The liquidity preference section on your term sheet can include a number of specifications, but will frequently have a multiple such as "1x," "2x," etc. This multiple determines the amount that must be paid back to your VC before anyone else gets a piece of the pie.

If you have a "1x" multiple (the standard), then your VC is guaranteed first pick at the company's liquidated assets in the event of a selloff or shutdown—up to the full amount they invested (they would have claim to twice what they invested with a "2x" multiplier, three times their investment with "3x," and so on). In the case of 1x, if your VC contributed $100k, and the company gets sold for $120k, they get their full $100k back (not a fraction of the sale price proportional to their equity). If the company sold for anything less than the VC's initial investment, they take everything. As a founder, you want to negotiate for this multiple to be low, if possible.

SAFE (simple agreement for future equity): A SAFE (Simple Agreement for Future Equity) is a type of agreement that is used to provide a company with funding in exchange for the promise of equity at a later date. SAFEs are similar to convertible notes in that they convert into equity at a later date, but they are simpler and have fewer terms than convertible notes.

SAFEs are typically used in the early stages of a company's development, when the company may not have a clear valuation or may not be ready to issue equity to investors. SAFEs are intended to provide companies with a flexible and simple way to raise capital without the need for a detailed equity round or the need to set a valuation for the company.

A SAFE typically includes a valuation cap (which sets the maximum value the company can reach before the notes convert to equity) and a conversion discount (a set discount from the current price of stock at the time of conversion). When SAFEs convert to equity, they do so at the lesser of the two prices created by the valuation cap and the conversion discount—thereby maximizing the shares the investor ends up with. SAFEs can also be implemented quickly and save you money on the legal fees associated with traditional fundraising rounds.

SAFEs don't represent current equity (they represent future equity if a triggering event occurs) in a company, and so don't typically give voting rights similar to common stock.

Related Entities: This refers to new businesses launched by the company or any of its founders or officers that are not owned directly by the company. Term sheets might include a clause specifying that if any related entities are created, the investor will automatically be issued stock in that venture as well.

Pro-Rata: A pro-rata clause is a provision in an agreement that allows an individual or entity to maintain a proportional ownership stake in a company by participating in future rounds of financing. For example, if an investor holds a 10% ownership stake in a company and the company subsequently raises additional funding through the sale of new shares, the pro-rata clause would allow the investor to purchase enough additional shares to maintain their 10% ownership stake. This would be achieved by allocating a portion of the new shares to the investor in proportion to their existing ownership stake.

Anti-Dilution: A dilution clause specifies whether the company can issue more shares in the future and under what conditions. Anti-dilution provisions can take several forms, but they generally operate by adjusting the conversion price of the investor's shares in the event that the company issues new shares at a lower price. This adjustment can be made either through a "full ratchet" provision, which adjusts the conversion price down to the new lower price, or through a "weighted average" provision, which adjusts the conversion price based on a formula that takes into account the number of new shares issued and the price at which they were issued. The terms may be different for different types of shares (preferred, common, deferred).

Most Favored Nation (MFN): an MFN clause is a term that gives the investor the right to inherit any terms offered in future fundraising rounds that are more favorable than those of the investor's initial buy-in.

Key Person: This term lays out that funding may be paused or canceled if a "key person" in the VC firm is unavailable. The investor may rely on key individuals, without whom their operations must be put on hold. If you have this clause on your term sheet, be aware that if that key person dies, quits, or otherwise doesn't have time to fully address the VC's investment in your company, the deal is off.

Investor Consent: This term specifies what (if any) company decisions must be approved by the investor, regardless of his/her percent ownership of the company. Typically, this is limited to decisions that are likely to directly affect the value of the investor's claim, such as issuing new stock, selling the company, or changes to the company's articles of incorporation or bylaws.

Information Rights: The law requires companies to provide their shareholders with various information about the state of the company. Beyond this, information rights entitle investors to receive further information about company financials and practices. This clause of the term sheet lists what (if any) information rights your VC will have.

Unissued Option Pool: An option pool is a portion of unallocated shares that can be distributed to employees and others down the road. This clause determines what happens if some of those shares go unused. This term might specify that unused options get redistributed proportionally to shareholders, are given to the VC, or any other arrangement.

Right of First Refusal: This is a right that investors may claim that applies to what happens when the company (or its founders) decide to sell shares to a third party. If investors have the right of first refusal, they are entitled to the opportunity to buy said shares before anyone else.

VC Legal Fees: VCs might make a company pay for the legal fees accrued by the VC while working on the deal. You can typically get a cap on spending of $10k - $25k for early-stage deals, which should be included in your term sheet.

LAWYER

Main points:

1. Hire an experienced lawyer to represent your interests and protect your rights.
2. Make sure to speak with the person who will be doing the work on a day-to-day basis, rather than just the initial contact at the firm.
3. Have an engagement letter in place that outlines the scope of work and fees schedule for your attorney.

Step 3: Get A Lawyer

Before you sign any documents or engage in negotiations for your term sheet, it is important to hire a lawyer who will represent your interests. Even if you have a good relationship with an investor, it is important to choose a lawyer who will be on your side and protect your rights. It is also advisable to find a lawyer through your own network, rather than using a lawyer recommended by someone who is not yet on your company's cap table. Be sure to interview and carefully consider your options before selecting a lawyer to ensure that you have the best representation for your business.

Look for a lawyer with experience both in your industry and in shepherding startups. Such lawyers will provide you with an engagement letter that both you and they will sign before representation begins. These letters (also called "fee agreements" or "retainer agreements") describe the scope of the work your attorney will do for you and the fees schedule you will pay.

Working with an attorney without an engagement letter can be dangerous because it can lead to misunderstandings and dissatisfaction. It's also a good idea to sign a disengagement letter once your work together is done so you have a clear end to the attorney-client relationship.

Lawyers typically bill in the $100 to $1,500+ per hour range, charged in 6 minute intervals. How much you'll pay for one depends on that firm you hire. On the least expensive end, you can hire solo practitioners. These can be just as experienced as any of the "big names" but charge a fraction of cost. In the middle are boutique firms (less than 20 attorneys). Legal bills can rack up quickly. Consider asking your lawyer to notify you when the bill has reached $3,000, so you can get a better understanding of how their billing works and so you are not stuck with a $50,000 legal bill after a few weeks of work. Keep in mind that much of the paperwork associated with starting a business is routine, easy work that most startup lawyers have done a hundred times so you don't need someone that can do legal gymnastics, someone that can do the work reliably will be fine

Ultimately, you're not hiring the firm, you're hiring the person doing the work at the firm. Make sure you get someone who knows what they're doing, even if they're at a big name firm.

Talk with the person that will be doing the work day to day, don't just talk to the partner that is your initial contact at the firm. It is unlikely that the partner will do any actual work so you want to talk to the person that will be doing the work day to day and make sure you have a good rapport with them and that they are competent.

How much you pay also depends on what fee structure you agree on. Many law firms will charge fixed-rate prices for various parts of the incorporation process, which is great for keeping legal bills from getting out of hand. If your deal requires more negotiation or is complex or unique for whatever reason, your attorney will probably prefer to bill at an hourly rate.

If you hire a law firm at an hourly rate, tell the firm to let you know when you have reached five hours, so you can get a better understanding of how the billing works (see Appendix B for an example of an itemized legal bill). This will also prevent you from getting an unexpectedly giant bill.

Many attorneys understand the entrepreneurial struggle of being cash poor and are willing to offer discounts if you negotiate for one. Getting a 10% off deal will save you hundreds, if not thousands, of dollars. It never hurts to ask (or play a little hard to get)!

You can also save by trusting your more mundane work to a paralegal or junior associate, as opposed to the partners of the company. Ask about this when you're looking around for a law firm to hire. Firms will often be able to specify the various billing rates for members of their team. Other tasks, such as notarizing documents, don't need to be done by your attorney and can instead be done online for cheap. Do some research so you know what services you need.

One more note about payment: Some firms will give you the option to defer payment for up to six months. Deferring payment can be useful, such as if you're still waiting on the VC's check to clear. A few firms may even accept stock in the company as payment. If either of these options are on the table, think carefully about the incentives they create. Deferred payments might cause you to be careless with your budgeting, or your lawyer to work inefficiently. Earning stock in the company might make your lawyer work harder, but could also lead to a conflict of interest between your interests and theirs.

Try to find a law firm that will defer payment at least until the completion of your first financing round—then you won't be stuck paying them out of pocket. Some firms, such as Wilmer Hale or Goodwin, for example, charge nothing until you've reached a fundraising milestone of $5 million. Other well-known firms that VCs have worked with in the past can also be helpful because of their reputations. The trade off is that these larger firms charge a lot more.

The good news is that once you're past the term sheet and getting a lawyer on your team, the incorporation process isn't as daunting.

PRE-INCORPORATION

Main points:

1. Setting up an entity and incorporating your business is important for protecting your personal assets and establishing your business as a separate legal entity.
2. Start to create a legal entity as things solidify with a VC to prevent delays.
3. Create a founders' agreement is a document that outlines the ownership and responsibilities of the founders in the business.

Before you can accept money from a VC, you need to set up an entity for your business. This is because venture capital investments are typically made into a business entity, rather than to an individual. Incorporating helps to protect your personal assets and establish your business as a separate legal entity.

However, incorporating can take a week or two to complete all of the necessary steps. You want to avoid the situation where a VC firm begins the process of drawing up documents for an investment, but your business is not yet incorporated. This can create delays and who knows what can happen because of the lost momentum or other extrinsic external factors.

To avoid these types of delays and complications, it is important to ensure that you have set up an entity and that the incorporation process is complete earlier rather than later. Before you can incorporate, in this chapter we will outline a number of things that you should do because they will be needed in the incorporation process.

Step 4: Craft (And Sign) A Founders' Agreement

If you're working alone, you can skip this step. If you are working with partners, founders, or anyone else who can claim a right to your product, you should begin by coming to an agreement about what future ownership and responsibilities will look like. This agreement should be written and signed by everyone.

Your founders' agreement will keep you and everyone else accountable throughout the incorporation process. Later, you will need to further formalize the points of this agreement in other corporate governing documents.

Some things you should include in your agreement are as follows:

1. Who the originators of various ideas and elements of your product are and to what extent these ideas and elements are being contributed to the company.
2. Who will be responsible for acting as the Incorporator (the person who files the paperwork needed to incorporate the company) and seeing the incorporation process through to completion.
3. Who will provide funding for the Incorporation phase (hiring lawyers, consultants, paying fees, etc.).
4. What ownership percentages will look like (50/50 is the easiest ownership split in cases with two co-owners, but be careful of voting deadlocks and consider ways to break ties, such as including a third seat on the board. You may also want the owner percentages to reflect contribution, which needn't be equal—consider what this will mean for how decisions are made).
5. What defines a founder. Early stage companies often have folks who join after the first two founders, but one may be producing or have a significant impact on the development of the company itself. Having a definition of "founder" can help avoid ill-will with early employees

and also reward those who do contribute at a founder level.

6. What happens if a co-owner wants to bow out of the venture at a later date. It's a good idea to add a vesting schedule to incentivize your co-founders to see the venture through to the end. You can either employ a gradual vesting schedule (each founder receives, say, 20% of their promised shares each year) or a vesting cliff. In the case of a cliff, the founders would receive nothing until a set date in the future, at which point they receive all their equity at once. Many firms set the founder vesting schedule based on time to motivate their founders to stick to the project, but some set vesting milestones in terms of company valuation to incentivize effort. For example, you and your co-founders could agree that you get your sellable shares only once the company is worth $100 million; if you work day and night and reach that valuation in a year, all the better.

When making this agreement, there are a few issues you should look out for. None of these are necessarily red flags, but how the owners will deal with them should be written down and agreed upon:

1. Are any partners/co-owners subject to prior agreements with a former employer? These could include non-compete or non-disclosure agreements as well as IP agreements from former employers. If a founder contributes IP that they created at their last job, their previous employer may try to claim part of your company.

2. Are there any assets that need to be transferred to the company?

3. Is IP licensed from a third party? Who is that IP currently licensed to? If such IP (or another permit,

license, etc.) is essential for the success of your product, what happens if the license is denied or becomes significantly more expensive?

4. Is the company or any of its members involved in any threatened or active litigation?

This is no means an exhaustive list, but it should get you thinking. The key is to work out as many details as possible with your partners before significant amounts of time and money are on the line.

Now that you have the basic agreement out of the way, there are a few easy things to do at this point that are fast, cheap, and that will save you time and money down the road.

Step 5: Set Up A Company Email

This can be a joint email for you and your partners or one for just you. You'll need it for virtually everything else you do throughout the incorporation process, and it's best to keep a record of your business communications in one place. Mixing private and business communication streams can cause lost leads and unpaid bills, legal and accounting nightmares, an unprofessional air, and transition issues when people leave the company or switch roles.

Step 6: Obtain A Virtual Mailing Address

For many legal and financial forms you will be filing out, you'll need a "physical address"where you can receive official mail to register your business. PO Boxes don't count and will be rejected by many forms automatically. If you have an office somewhere, great! If not, you can sign up for a "virtual mailing address". A virtual mailing address is a remote location your business uses to receive mail without you having to live or work there.

Unfortunately, most states (including Delaware) don't accept PO boxes for incorporation addresses. What you can do instead is take advantage of virtual mailbox companies such as SnapMail (snapmailbox.com) or iPostal1 (iPostal1.com) that provide you with a "physical address" and then scan and email, shred, or forward your mail based on your request.

Using a virtual mailbox requires you to sign a form that authorizes the company to receive and open your mail. You can do this by filling out a USPS 1583 form, which will be required by whatever virtual mailing company you go with.

The 1583 form needs to be notarized to prove your identity. You can find a notary at your local courthouse, bank, UPS, or by looking up notaries in your area (though call ahead because notaries aren't always there during all business hours). These usually charge a small fee ($20 or so). For any of these locations, make sure to call ahead to get the exact hours the notary will be there that day.

Thanks to webcams, many online notaries also exist. Companies such as NotaryCam (notarycam.com) will notarize your document from anywhere in the world through a video chat. They charge a bit more than a local notary, but you never have to leave the house.

Step 7: Obtain A Virtual Phone Number

Virtual phone services can be obtained from companies that provide cloud-based phone systems. They enable you to receive calls from anywhere using your laptop or phone. Having an official business phone number adds credibility to your business —as opposed to sending callers to your personal number. Find a provider you like, get a main business number (and others for you and your partners, if you'd like), and set up your voicemail. If you use Gmail, Google Voice is free for personal use and has a business integration that starts at just $6/month.

Step 8: Apply For An Ein

An EIN (employer identification number) is a federally issued code needed to open a bank account, get a business license, work with vendors, and, like the name implies, hire employees. The application process is simple, and the IRS website has instructions to walk you through it. Go here to get started: irs.gov/businesses/small-businesses-self-employed/apply-for-an-employer-identification-number-ein-online

Step 9: Set Up A Bank Account

You need a company bank account to accept the money from your VC, so it's a good idea to get this out of the way so it doesn't hold you up later.

A few of the more popular banks for startups are Mercury, First Republic, and Silicon Valley Bank (SVB), though most any bank will do. In my experience, Mercury has been good. Check the interest rates when signing up because you will be getting a significant amount of money from the VC and it is nice to be able to earn interest on it if possible.

Step 10: Apply For A Credit Card

Your business needs to build a credit history just like you do. Beyond building credit, a business credit card makes it easy to pay for miscellaneous things like travel and meetings without any liquidity constraints.

The best companies for getting your first company credit card are Brex, Ramp, and Divvy. These companies analyze your startup's funding and performance to determine your credit limit. This is a huge advantage because you can quickly open a significant line of credit without needing a long credit history, which your business doesn't have at this point.

With these easy steps out of the way, you're now ready to proceed with incorporation.

INCORPORATION

Main points:

1. Incorporation protects business owners from personal liability.
2. Delaware C Corp is a popular choice for incorporation.
3. Services like Clerky can help with the incorporation process.

Incorporating gives you protection and organization by creating a legal entity that is separate from its owners. Your company can then own property, employ others, and do similar things that an individual can do. It can also be sued and held liable for debts, which is where the legal protection is important.

One of the main reasons to incorporate is that, by establishing the business as separate from its founders, you put a legal barrier between you and the company. If your company capsizes or gets sued, you (probably) won't be personally liable.

However, business entities protect their owners from liability in almost all situations; they don't give you a pass for negligence or unlawful conduct, so don't do anything your parents wouldn't approve of.

Step 11: Pick The Right Entity

You've probably heard of terms like "LLC," "S Corp," "LLP," and so on. These stand for different types of business entities. The first step to filing your own is determining which type of legal entity is right for your business.

Everyone starts out as a sole proprietor or a general partnership; these are the legal default options. Sole proprietors and partnerships have no legal protection, but they also don't need their owners to do anything to be created. You have a sole proprietorship if you're conducting business by yourself and haven't incorporated yet, and you're a partnership if you're doing so jointly with someone else. The law sees no difference between the sole proprietor / partners and their business.

As you may imagine, things need to change once an investor wants to buy part of the operation. The main entity type you have to choose from include the following:

1. Corporation
2. Limited Liability Partnership
3. Limited Partnership
4. Limited Liability Company

A startup can also be a non-profit 501c(3) if its purpose is scientific, educational, or charitable. One benefit of filing as a non-profit is the tax-exempt status that goes along with it. This is outside the scope of the book but explore it more if your startup fits in the above categories.

One more option is to look into incorporating as a Public Benefit Corporation (PBC, also known as a B Corp). PBCs can go public and have all the benefits of regular corporations but are inseparably tied to their non-monetary mission (e.g., "produce clean energy for all"). PBCs are similar in some ways to non-profit companies, but can still turn a taxable profit.

Which entity is right for you depends on several factors. You should think about these four main points when making the decision:

1. The projected size of your company (in revenue and employees)
2. The number and value of assets you plan to develop or

hold
3. The risk in your industry (construction or medical research companies are more likely to get sued for accidents than consultancies, for example)
4. Whether you plan to eventually take your company public

A limited liability partnership (LLP) is a partnership in which the partners are not personally liable for the debts of the partnership. This means that the partners' personal assets, such as their homes and savings, are protected in the event that the partnership incurs debts that it is unable to pay. LLPs are often used by professional service firms, such as law firms and accounting firms.

A limited partnership (LP) is a partnership in which there are one or more general partners, who are personally liable for the debts of the partnership, and one or more limited partners, who are not personally liable for the debts of the partnership. Limited partners typically do not participate in the management of the partnership, and their liability is limited to the amount of their investment in the partnership.

A limited liability company (LLC) is a business structure that combines the liability protection of a corporation with the tax benefits of a partnership. LLCs are owned by members, who are not personally liable for the debts of the LLC. The members of an LLC are able to choose how the LLC will be taxed, either as a partnership or as a corporation.

These entities are lightweight and easy to file—perfect for "Mom-n-Pop" businesses—but you need something more robust if you're hoping your startup will eventually become larger.

Since this book is for entrepreneurs who anticipate securing venture funding, the best option is most likely a corporation so that you have maximum protection.

Corporations are run by a board of directors. The board sets direction of the company, hires and fires the CEO, and approves certain high-level decisions about budgeting, partnerships, and initiatives. In the startup stage, the board of directors is usually just the founder(s) themselves.

Ownership of a corporation is typically measured in shares of stock (as opposed to membership). These shareholders elect the board of directors and have the right to vote on issues like issuing new stock or selling the company.

On a day-to-day level, corporations are run by officers. Many states require corporations to maintain a minimum number of officers, such as a president, a treasurer, and a secretary. These roles may be filled by the same person. These officers answer to the board and are bound by its decisions.

Corporations can take on debt, enter into contracts, and sue/be sued without members being personally liable. They are ultimately governed by state and federal law, as well as by the legal documents their founders create, such as bylaws (more on this in the next chapter).

Step 12: Elect Your Tax Status

Most corporations are filed as "C Corporations" (C-Corps). This is the most common tax status, and the one I focus on in this book. C Corps pay taxes on profits, and then their shareholders pay income tax on dividends.

Special corporations can file as "S Corporations" (S-Corps). These companies do not pay taxes on profits; instead, profits are automatically passed through to the shareholders/owners, who report total profits/losses on their personal income statements. This is also the tax treatment that partnerships (general and LLP) have.

In a way, filing as an S-Corp gives you a tax advantage in that you are not "double taxed" (on profits and dividends). The downsides to S-Corps include the following:

1. You can't use an S-Corp to shelter your wealth from taxes down the road,
2. You can't have more than 100 equity holders,
3. You can't have more than one class of equity (which means you can't have both common and preferred stock),
4. No non-human (aka another business) can hold equity in the company.

It turns out that for most large startups, the best option is to file as a C-Corp.

Step 13: Pick A State To File In

All business entities are filed on the state level. Consequently, the process for incorporating and the requirements for doing so vary depending on which state you file in. And no, you don't have to file in the state where you live or intend to have your business headquarters. You still have to pay taxes in whatever states you do business in, but you might want to incorporate in a different state because some states are more business-friendly (lower taxes) than others.

One of those states is Delaware. In fact, angel investors and VCs overwhelmingly prefer that you file in Delaware because it gives large companies tax advantages and Delaware courts tend to rule very corporation friendly.

In some cases (especially for small to mid-sized businesses), filing in your home state is the most cost-efficient option. You'll have to at least register your business in each state you actively do business in anyway.

Wyoming and Utah are becoming a strong contender for crypto-based companies. In particular, Wyoming is the first state to recognize blockchain stock and exempts utility tokens from security laws, which is very important for fundraising with crypto (if you're looking at creating a crypto company, skip ahead to the crypto chapter).

For that reason, the steps in this chapter are based on Delaware law, but the process is similar in other states.

Step 14: Obtain A Registered Agent

Delaware (and other states) requires you to have a registered agent. The agent is no more than a person with an address in Delaware who is responsible for collecting legal notices on behalf of your company. You or your law firm can hire a company (usually a CPA) to provide this service for a small yearly fee or you can hire one yourself.

Step 15: Reserve A Legal Name For Your Business

Your business can present itself under many different brands and names, but it needs a legal title to go on official documents. Talk to your team and get a respectable name for your company, then register it on the state business registration website (for Delaware, go to: icis.corp.delaware.gov/Ecorp/NameReserv/NameReservation.aspx).

Once you've brainstormed a few names, check them against other registered trademarks and company names (yours must be unique, after all). The easiest way to do this is to use the federal Trademark Electronic Search System (TESS, tmsearch.uspto.gov).

Keep in mind that the company name must include a valid corporate suffix. These are the most popular:

1. Incorporated
2. Inc.
3. Corporation
4. Corp.

Also note that your business name should not include the words "trust" or "bank."

Step 16: File A Certificate Of Incorporation

The Certificate of Incorporation is what gets you officially incorporated (once it's accepted) and is the single most important document of this whole process. In Delaware, filing one is easy. You can submit the required information on the state website, and a plethora of online companies can help you get this done if you're looking for guidance such as: Clerky (clerky.com) or FirstBase (firstbase.io)

You will be required to submit the following information:

1. The title of the company,
2. The location of the company's registered workplace within the state and the company's registered agent's name,
3. A statement of issuable stocks, their type and value, and
4. The title and addresses of the company's incorporator(s).

The statement of issuable stocks is a short document that sets a limit to the number of stocks the company can offer, explains your general plan for distributing them, and mentions what the approximate value of those shares is.

The number of shares the company issues needn't be the maximum amount you list in your statement. In fact, it's a good idea not to issue all of them at once.

Many experts recommend setting your authorized stock limit at 10 million. An example of your statement of issuable stocks could look like this:

Number of Shares of Common Stock Authorized: 10,000,000. Estimated Value Share Value: $0.0001.

Company Stock Issuance Plan:

1. Retain 1,000,000 shares for future distribution to employees, consultants, advisors, and directors as part of compensation and incentive plans.
2. Retain 1,000,000 shares to be unissued, except for necessary fundraising (sold on the market).
3. Issue 8,000,000 shares to the company founders following incorporation, subject to a vesting schedule.

Once your Certificate of Incorporation has been approved by the state, your registered agent will receive (and forward on to you) documentation confirming your incorporation.

Step 17: What It Costs And How To Do It Cheaply

All in costs for incorporating a company will be $5,000 - $20,000 in for a seed round. Most of this will be spent on lawyers. The actual incorporation can be done for $2,000-$5,000 using a service , which I recommend using. I found Clerky (clerky.com) to be excellent. Other services that offer similar service are Stripe Atlas (stripe.com) and Firstbase (firstbase.io).

The legal fees will come from needing the lawyer to review one-off contracts, write the bylaws, help the board ratify documents, and other questions that come up along the way. It is easy to rack up a high legal bill with even one 8 hour day. You may pay less or more depending on how much work you do yourself and how much you rely on professionals. If you go on to a Series A fundraising round or beyond, you're looking to pay $20,000 - $50,000+ in legal fees.

It may seem like a decent chunk of money, but having a lawyer that knows what they are doing will help to prevent any mistakes. While hiring a lawyer who is a family friend or acquaintance may seem like a more cost-effective or convenient option, it is important to remember that they may not have the expertise or experience needed to do corporate formation work.

For those with less time but who want to save on startup costs there are also a few great companies that streamline the creation of all the documents you need. Some also provide you with a registered agent as well. These online services can help you generate legal code for a fraction of the normal cost.

You may find yourself wondering if jumping through all the hoops is worth it. You'll thank yourself down the road for taking care of these things now.

POST-INCORPORATION

Main points:

1. Establish the structure and operation of the corporation through bylaws.
2. Appoint initial board of directors and appoint company officers.
3. Complete an 83(b) election for founders to minimize tax liability on early stock grants.

So, your company has been incorporated in Delaware. Now what? If incorporating is like buying a new computer—you've researched, selected, and obtained a powerful tool—this next phase of business development is like setting up the software on that computer to meet your needs. A generic corporation sounds impressive, but it isn't very useful until you've customized it.

Step 18: Write And Adopt Bylaws

Bylaws are the rules that govern the company (think of them like a constitution for your business). Writing and adopting bylaws is an important step in the process of incorporating a business because it establishes the structure and operation of the corporation. It allows the company to define its own policies and procedures, rather than having to follow default rules set by state law. This can be particularly important for companies that have unique business models or that operate in specialized industries. Adopting bylaws also helps to ensure that the corporation is run in a transparent and accountable manner. The bylaws should outline the procedures for holding meetings, making decisions, and handling financial matters, which helps to prevent conflicts of interest and ensure that the corporation is run in the best interests of all stakeholders.

Good bylaws should include the following:

1. A statement of purpose that explains why you are in business, what your business does (generally), who your primary customers are, what makes you unique, etc.
2. What the duties of the board are and how members are appointed to it.
3. How board meetings will run and how they will be called.
4. If a board meeting can be called without the CEO and what is the threshold for which a board meeting can be called
5. How the board will vote (what constitutes a quorum, etc.) and what requires board approval.
6. Procedures for dealing with conflicts of interest among board members.
7. Indemnification of board members.
8. How directors and officers of the company are elected and how long they are appointed.
9. What (if any) core committees will exist among the board and their purpose.
10. How stock is initially distributed and the rules for buying and selling it.
11. When and how often shareholder meetings will occur.
12. What the shareholder voting requirements are.
13. The process for amending the bylaws.

Something you might consider writing into the bylaws is a stipulation that the CEO can only be fired for a good reason, "for cause", and consider giving a definition for this term. You don't want to end up like Steve Jobs—at least not in the sense of being fired from your own company. Consider also stipulating in the bylaws that the board can't meet or vote on anything without the CEO in attendance.

Another option to consider including in the bylaws is a provision for founder transfers, which allows founders to transfer their ownership stakes in the company to others. This can be useful in situations such as when a founder wishes to sell their stake or when a founder leaves the company and wants to transfer their ownership to a new team member.

You'll need to think through what the bylaws should say and then have someone else (an attorney, for example) write it up. If you don't have an attorney and want to save money, you can draft bylaws yourself while using Clerky—while making minor modifications if you need to—and then have an expert review it at the end. The final product should be a formal document the board can vote to adopt.

Step 19: Establish A Board Of Directors

Once the bylaws are complete, it's time to get a board. Follow the procedure specified in your bylaws and get the right people on your executive team.

This typically is done through something called an Actions of Incorporator, which is a document that outlines the actions you take as the incorporator once your business is incorporated but before you have a board. The main purpose of this document is to adopt the bylaws for the corporation and appoint the initial board of directors. Once you've executed a document that does that, your absolute power as incorporator ends and you can move on to working with your team.

When you set up a board, make sure you don't give up control of your company at the same time. As the CEO, you have to answer to the board for everything you do. If the board is full of people with a significantly different vision than you, you might find yourself unable to steer your company to meet your vision.

One thing you should be aware of is that seats on the board don't have to have equal voting power. You can write your position on the board extra votes into your bylaws. Such positions on the board are called "supervoting seats." You can also have "supervoting shares."

Those precautions are for worst-case scenarios. From day one, you should choose a board of people who are trustworthy and aligned with your vision. It's also important that your board has the expertise that you need to scale your company. You want an investor who doesn't just contribute money but also connections and wisdom to help you and the company to grow efficiently and effectively.

In some cases, the board of directors may be divided into two classes: common directors and preferred directors. Common directors are elected by all of the shareholders of the company and represent the interests of all shareholders. Preferred directors, on the other hand, are elected by a specific class of shareholders and typically represent the interests of that class.

In a common vs preferred director vote, the common directors are typically voted on by all of the shareholders of the company, while the preferred directors are voted on by a specific class of shareholders. This means that the common directors are responsible for representing the interests of all shareholders, while the preferred directors are responsible for representing the interests of a specific class of shareholders.

One reason a company might use a common vs preferred director vote is to give certain shareholders more influence over the board of directors. For example, a company might have a class of preferred shareholders who have invested a larger amount of money in the company and therefore have a greater stake in its success. These preferred shareholders might be given the ability to elect a preferred director who will represent their interests on the board of directors.

Step 20: Appoint Directors And Officers

Elect or appoint your C-Suite leadership by following your bylaws. In some cases, all of those roles will be covered by a single person. These roles are bound to adapt as time goes on, but they should be generally outlined in writing either by you or by the board.

Step 21: Sign Founder Ip Agreements

Every company has intellectual property it wants to protect —and so do many individuals. An IP agreement (also known as Proprietary Information and Inventions Assignment Agreements (PIIAAs) or Confidential Information and Inventions Assignment Agreements (CIIAAs)) delineate what intellectual property the company has rights to and what is owned by various members of the company.

Typically, any IP (including patents, copyrights, trademarks, etc.) created before joining the company is retained by individuals, and anything created while working for the company is company property, but you can agree on whatever fits your needs best. Effective agreements also include clauses that list nondisclosure, non-solicitation, and noncompetition policies.

Step 22: Sign A Restricted Stock Purchase Agreement

You may decide, along with the other founders, to put rules on the amount of new stock issued and what buyers can do with it. A Restricted Stock Purchase Agreement is a document, signed by the founders, that sets forth the rights of stockholders and vesting schedules. Your agreement could put limits on when or in what quantity shareholders can sell or transfer their shares, give the company the right to buy back shares, refuse or prevent certain sales, issue new shares, etc.

Stock can be a powerful business tool and an investment that can make you rich, but it can also cause headaches for your company down the road if the proper agreements aren't in place. Talk to your team (including investors, if they are receiving shares) and get their input, then have your lawyer write it down and get everyone to sign it.

Step 23: Issue Stock To The Founders

Based on the bylaws, you should now issue official stock to the founders.

Although not required, I recommend that you have every founder vest their stock. This prevents co-founders from walking away from the company six months in with a massive amount of equity.

Each founder should deliver a check to the company for the stock (dated with the purchase date). You should then deposit this check in the company's bank account, and keep a photocopy of the checks in the company's files. It's also a very good idea to start keeping a record of all transactions now—from day one—for your future accounting and legal purposes and to provide all payers with a receipt.

To issue stock, you should provide the recipients with a Notice of Stock Issuance. This document serves in place of old-school paper stock certificates. The purpose of the notice is to confirm investors and founders of their stock holding. This can be done with Carta and Pulley.

Additionally, make sure you specify what, if any, legal roles or privileges the spouses of founders have in stock decisions.

Step 24: Get Founders To Complete An 83(B)

Election

An 83(b) election tells the IRS how you prefer to be taxed on your stock equity. You can either elect to pay income tax on the share value now (when you receive the stock) or later when the stock vests—which is always at least a year in the future.

Each stock recipient must make an 83(b) election by filing the necessary paperwork with (and sending a letter to) the IRS within 30 days. It is very important not to miss this deadline because the IRS does not grant exceptions. Specifically, you (and each other stock recipient) will need to do the following:

1. Download the Section 83(b) Election and Instructions document from the IRS website.
2. Fill out four copies of the form (it's a one-pager).
3. Mail two copies to the IRS by USPS Certified Mail. Include a self-addressed, postage-paid envelope and request that the IRS send one form (stamped with the date) back to you for your records.
4. File one copy with the company records.
5. Keep one copy for yourself.

Step 25: Official Close On The Venture Funding

No matter how good your fundraising prospects look, nothing is official until contracts are signed (physically inked or signed with a verified online contract service such as DocuSign and PandaDoc). Keep your fundraising efforts going until you get signatures and until the money is in your bank account.

Step 26: Issue Stock To Everyone Else

For tax reasons, you want to complete issuing founder stock and the 83(b) Election before you issue stock to your investors and whomever else is entitled to it. Once you get to this point, use notices of stock issuance and keep good records, just like you did for issuing stock to the founders.

POST-FUNDRAISING

Main points:

1. File a Form D exemption with the SEC within 15 days after the first sale of your first security offering.
2. Get a 409A valuation to determine the fair market value of the company's stock for purposes of setting the exercise price of stock options.
3. Maintain an up-to-date cap table to accurately reflect the ownership and equity structure of the company.

The money from you, your partners, and your VC has cleared in your new company checking account. Now what? Well, don't jump to business just yet. You still have one more stage to get through before you start hiring. For starters, you need to register with the federal government.

Step 27: File A Form D

What the term sheet described above is selling a portion of your company. This is known as security by the government. When selling a security, the government wants to make sure you're not swindling people who don't have much investing experience. Depending on the complexity of the security that is being sold, the government has different filing requirements.

A Form D, also known as the Notice of Sale of Securities, is required by law to privately sell stock in your company (if you're offering stock publicly, that requires a whole process of its own). It requires you to disclose basic information about the officers and owners in the company, the stock offering, and the business generally.

Registering your stock sale is generally required, but many companies are exempt from the registration if they fall within certain criteria (some of the most common of which are listed below). Even if your company is exempt from the Form D registration, you still have to file a notice of exception to the SEC within 15 days after the first sale of your first security offering.

How seriously you take this step depends on your risk level. Many entrepreneurs don't register fundraising when they are using a SAFE, they think that selling "the promise of future equity" does not count as selling equity. However, in my research, SAFEs are securities and are subject to state and federal law. My recommendation, if you are using a SAFE or convertible note, is to get a lawyer and have them figure out which exception you fall under. Here are the most common exemptions.

1. Limited Offerings - Rule 504. This exception applies if you sell less than $10 million of securities in a 12-month period. It does not apply if you are starting an investment company, intend to immediately merge or acquire an unidentified company, don't have a business plan, or have been in trouble with the SEC in the past.
2. Private Placements - Rule 506(b). If you have less than 35 non-accredited investors, each of those investors have substantial experience in finance and business and have been thoroughly informed about this particular investment, there has been no attempt to publicly advertise the investment opportunity, and the investors agree to not publicly resell their shares, then you may qualify for this exception.
3. General Solicitation - Rule 506(c). This exception makes it possible to publicly advertise and widely solicit the chance to invest in your company so long as you screen all potential investors and ensure they meet the "accreditation" level. Note that the stock you sell under

this exception must count as "restricted securities" that are not freely tradable.

4. Regulation A - Tier 1. This option allows you to raise up to $20 million in a 12-month period. The filing process requires you to get approval from the SEC and the state department, but your financial statements do not have to be audited.

5. Regulation A - Tier 2. This option is similar to Tier 1, but you can raise $75 million in a 12-month period and while you still have to file with the SEC, you do not have to file with the state. The downside is that some of your financial statements must be audited by an independent accountant to qualify.

Again, it's best to talk to a professional about which exception is best for you—they might even tell you to register your offering with the SEC instead.

As soon as the money clears or papers are signed with your VC, get online, and file a Form D with the SEC (or ask your lawyer to do it and skip the rest of this step). You can file this form before selling securities, so feel free to take care of it earlier if you wish.

Keep in mind that the 15-day deadline is a strict one. Filing the form is free, but you do have to have it notarized.

One more note, you can technically file with the state instead of the federal government. Because the federal system is both easy to use and less expensive, many entrepreneurs avoid filing on the state level. One benefit to registering with the state is that you may not have to disclose the amount of money you raised (or intend to raise). Making that data public could either scare away competitors or encourage them, so if you're worried about that, talk to a professional.

You will need to file the form using the Fed's Electronic Data Gathering, Analysis and Retrieval system (EDGAR, sec.gov/edgar.shtml). This will require you to use your business' Central

Index Key (CIK), which is given to you when you register your business on EDGAR. You will need to have basic information about your business ready, as well as your business EIN.

Since it may take a few days to get registered with EDGAR (you have to apply and get approved), don't wait until day fourteen to get this done.

Step 28: Get Board Approval

While any fundraising up to this point was probably secured through deliberation with your partners—or with yourself if you're the sole founder—you are now subject to the board and the company bylaws. If you have plans to continue with another round of fundraising (now or in the future), you will need to get official approval by the board. Technically, you also needed board approval to get your current VC on board in the first place.

Board approval is an important part of securing indemnification for yourself against lawsuits from unhappy investors down the road. Board indemnification doesn't absolve you of all responsibility, but if you go rogue and get fundraising without official board approval, you can potentially get into a lot of trouble.

"But what if we created the board *after* securing VC funding?" you ask.

This issue can be solved by having the board ratify the previous actions you took to found the company and acquire the necessary capital. Doing so is easy. Just have your board meet and vote on it (while keeping minutes of the proceedings), or better yet, have all the board members sign a document ratifying your actions.

You can actually complete this step as soon as you've incorporated (even if you don't have a board yet), because under Delaware law, the default is that you (the Incorporator) are the board unless specified otherwise.

Step 29: Create And Manage A Cap Table

A capitalization table (or "cap table") is a table that keeps track of all the stock, notes, warrants, and equity grants your company owns or has ever issued. It's basically an accounting list of where all the company equity is.

Keeping this table updated is critical. You can use a basic spreadsheet, or you can take advantage of software specifically designed to help you manage your cap table.

Recommended cap table software:

1. Carta (carta.com)
2. Pulley (pulley.com)

Step 30: Establish An Employee Equity Plan

As a startup, your company will probably need to offer stock options to attract top talent. Before you start throwing numbers around with potential employees, you and the board need to establish an employee equity plan.

Start with the number of shares you set aside for employee incentives during the Incorporation phase (in your statement of issuable stocks). That's what you have to work with.
Consider the culture you want to promote in your company and think of ways to use stock options to incentivize that culture. Take your plan to the board and vote on it together (typically, the CEO makes options recommendations, and the board approves them). Be careful that you don't immediately burn through all your issuable stock; you'll want to hire more people in the future, so it's best to reserve a large portion of issuable securities for later.

That said, early-stage companies have little cash, loads of equity, and need to move fast. You can attract high-performance employees early in the game with a low salary if you offer significant equity (+1%) that will vest after a specified time or once the company reaches a certain valuation target.

Once you have your plan in place, you can start granting shares to your employees (within the bounds of the next step). Be sure to keep everything official and specify in the employment contract and/or the equity certificate how soon the stock can be vested.

Step 31: Get A 409A Valuation

There is an important restriction on the "exercise price" of stock options that you should know about. The "exercise price" (also known as the "strike price") is a locked-in price at which option holders (such as your employees) can buy stock when they choose to exercise their option.

The restriction comes from section 409A of the Internal Revenue Code. It penalizes you for issuing options with an exercise price lower than the fair market value of the stock when the option is granted. For example, if your stock is currently worth $10 a share, you can't promise your employee that they can buy it in the future for $8.

To ensure that your company doesn't get in trouble with the IRS in the future, get a qualified independent appraiser to issue you a "409A Valuation," which pinpoints your stock value on a particular date. When you get a valuation, you can use it to set the minimum price of any stock you issue for one year from the date of valuation (unless something happens sooner that would materially change the value of your company). Also note that if you got a valuation before fundraising, you will need to get another one, as VC funding counts as a material change in the value of your company.

These valuations can cost between $1,000 - $10,000, depending on the complexity of your company, and can take a few weeks. You can technically create the valuation yourself, but doing so is very risky. Having a 409a Valuation created by an experienced professional will be enough to prove that your stock issuance was in line with the law if you ever need to.

Step 32: 409A Data Request

When you hire an accountant to put a 409A valuation together for you (Carta and Pulley can do this as well), you will need to provide them with a number of documents. In addition, your accountant will also ask you questions about your business plan and associated risks, your team, your future fundraising plans, and your run rate.

The information requested might also include:

1. Historical financial statements for up to five years (as available). These consist of an income statement and balance sheet.
2. Year-to-date financial statements for the current year.
3. Financial projections for the next one to five years, as available.
4. Your cap table as of the valuation date, including an options ledger with your proposed exercise prices.
5. The company's Articles/Certificate of Incorporation.
6. Recent board/investor materials or other management-level presentations that provide a snapshot of the company's status and plans.
7. The estimated number of options expected to be granted in the next 12 months.
8. Copies of any past 409A valuation reports.

You should use Quickbooks or Xero to generate many of these reports so you don't have to do them manually.

From there, the 409a assessor will do an initial data review, then likely meet with you to get more information. Then comes the analysis and final evaluation.

Getting a 409A valuation can seem like an arduous ordeal, but it's valuable from a management perspective as well as a legal perspective because it helps entrepreneurs make sure their financial ducks are all in a row.

Once you get your 409A from the accountant, you will need to get it approved by the board. Use those numbers when offering stock options and keep the document safe somewhere in case your legal team needs to use it.

Step 33: Sign Advisor Agreements

If you have any official advisors or consultants to whom you owe securities, draw up and sign an Advisor Agreement. These agreements outline the bounds and duration of the services they will provide, their compensation, their relationship to the company (e.g., contractor), and specifications about IP and nondisclosure that protect your company assets and information.

These agreements tend to be pretty standard, so I recommend using a template from a company such as Clerky or the Founder Institute (fi.co). Like the employee equity plan, update your cap table whenever you issue new equity and be careful about issuing so much that you inhibit the company from issuing more in the future.

Step 34: File Beneficial Ownership

"Beneficial owners" are people who own a significant share of the company's equity. Anyone who acquires 5% or more of the company's shares must file a Schedule 13D with the SEC. You'll need to file this yourself, and informing your teammates and investors about it will save them from tax trouble down the road and keep your business professional.

This schedule should be filed within 10 days of the acquisition.

Clerky (and many other online services) can help you put this together. Ultimately, you'll need to file the schedule with EDGAR.

And that's it! You're finally done with the legal follow-up from your fundraising efforts.
Onward to hiring!

HIRING

Main points:

1. Consider whether new hires will be classified as employees or contractors.
2. Offer letters are an important way to formally document the terms of the employment relationship.
3. Before offering equity to potential hires, make sure to have board approval and consider the blend of equity, commission, and salary that will be most attractive to the type of team members you are seeking.

Employees vs contractors | Writing offer letters and employment contracts | Complying with employee tax and withholding laws | Paying your people

The moment you've been waiting for has arrived: it's time to hire your team!

As far as recruitment goes, top talent can be competitive. Here are two services that help you contact and build relationships with potential employees:

1. AngelList Talent (angel.co) - a recruitment platform specializing in talent for startups.
2. Gem (gem.com) - a Chrome extension for automating cold reach outs and follow ups.
3. LinkedIn (linkedin.com)

Once you've recruited the right people, you can get them on your payroll in a few easy steps.

Step 35: Identify Employee Vs. Contractor Positions

Employers have a legal responsibility to take care of their employees by paying taxes for them and providing them with benefits, tools, training, vacation time, and so on. They do not have the same obligation to contractors.

Independent contractors are treated as separate businesses. This means that you can pay contractors for their work and move on with your life without the hassle of being a true employer. On the flip side, it can be harder to align incentives with contractors by compensating them with equity on the same level as employees.

A middle ground for those who need employee work done but prefer to build up their HR department later is Professional Employer Organizations. These organizations employ professionals and lease their services out to companies. The PEO will then take care of most of the HR-related business pertaining to said professionals, leaving you to focus on developing and selling your product.

Another benefit to hiring using a PEO is that it makes international recruitment and having an office in another country easy, which might be higher quality and less expensive than getting the same level of talent in your location. The downside is that these employees bill at a slightly higher rate than you would have to pay them to work for you directly (you're basically hiring an HR department on top of the workers, after all).

One PEO that I have found to work well is Deel (letsdeel.com).

Step 36: Send Offer Letters

Calling your winning candidates is a must. Sending them official offer letters is also a must. These letters communicate your job offer and add a level of professionality to the deal that many of the best employees expect. Even more importantly, these letters protect your company by formally documenting the agreed-upon terms of the employment relationship. You don't want an employee claiming they were promised more than what you agreed to.

In the letter, reiterate your basic terms (compensation, job role, remote/location policy, relocation reimbursement, etc.) as well as your hiring decision.

There are three main types of compensation that you'll have to decide between when attracting talent: salary, commission/bonuses, and equity. Your mix of the three should match both your budget and the interests of the type of people you want on your team.

Offering more equity, for example, tends to attract people who are more risk prone and creates powerful incentives for those team members to see the company succeed. But offering too little cash up front may make it hard to get experienced professionals on board (who have lots of other more stable job opportunities). Similarly, commissions can be very motivating.

Make sure you're clear about the blend of equity, commission, and salary you are proposing in your offer letter—and before that in your recruiting and interviews. Also remember that promising equity isn't something the CEO can do alone; any transfer of equity requires board approval once the employee agreement has been signed.

What you should offer as a compensation package varies a lot based on the required skill set, experience, and location. You can research current salaries and equity shares at AngelList Talent (angel.co/salaries) to get an idea of what the market is currently offering.

Generally, your equity offering should be higher for your very first employees and taper off over time. Early employees are taking a risk working for an unknown entity. Be sure to plan this progression out so you don't run out of equity too soon.

Step 37: Create (And Sign) Employment Contracts

For every position you hire for, create an employment contract. Each new employee should sign his/her contract before doing any work for you. Don't allow work to begin before the contract is signed.

Employment contracts have no set structure and can be almost whatever you want them to be (the only restriction is that the job requirements must align with the Federal Fair Labor Standards and any applicable laws in the state where you do business), but thorough employment contracts typically include the following elements:

1. **At-will and termination**: this section states that employment is for an indefinite period of time (unless it's not—then specify) and may be terminated either by employer or employee.
2. **Benefits**: If your company provides a 401k match, paid time off, maternity/paternity leave, vacation time, or any form of insurance (health, dental, life, etc.), the agreement should specify what, how much, and any conditions that must be met to receive those benefits. If your company does not provide any benefits (many startups do not), the agreement should say so.
3. **Good faith**: This section states that the employee agrees to put forth his/her best efforts and describes any severance package or policy you will provide. It should also note that the employee will not bring to the job (illegally) any IP from his/her previous employer.
4. **Communications**: this section discusses whether the company requires the employee to use specific

communication outlets (company email, phone, etc.) and to what extent the company owns and/or will monitor work-related communications.

5. **Responsibilities**: This part lists the general roles and duties the person is hired for, his/her official title, and to whom he/she reports. It's okay to note that the exact responsibilities are subject to change; just make sure that the person knows that startups require team members to wear multiple hats on occasion.

6. **Schedule**: Here you should specify when the employee is expected to work and how many hours a week are required. Stating that overtime may occasionally be required is also a good idea (working for a startup is anything but having a boring nine-to-five).

7. **Compensation**: Be clear here about your proposed salary, bonuses or commission (and the related requirements), and stock options. If stock is included, be sure to specify the type (typically "restricted/deferred") and the vesting period.

8. **Clawback**: A clawback provision specifies conditions under which the company can take back incentives, bonuses, or stock options previously given to employees (perhaps for violating the employment agreement, quitting prematurely, etc.) You don't want your employees to have the option of making off with a share of your company for a week's worth of work.

9. **Confidentiality**: adding a nondisclosure term is a great idea for protecting your IP and business systems from competition in the future.

10. **Inventions assignment**: If your employee will be developing or inventing tools, procedures, or products, this section should state that any industry-relevant inventions (IP) created while the employee is working for you belong to the company. These stipulations are often found in Confidential Information and Invention Assignment Agreements (CIIAA) or Proprietary

Information and Invention Assignment Agreements (PIIAA) independent of employment contracts. Whether you have a separate agreement or work this term into the employment contract is up to you; the important thing is that you establish a contractual right to your company's future IP.

11. **Non-competition**: If not included in your CIIAA or PIIAA, add a section to the agreement that specifies whether the employee is permitted to work for another company in the same industry while working for you.

12. **Non-solicitation**: This section restricts the relationships the employee may have with the company's clients or customers. In essence, the employee agrees not to solicit those clients or customers for their own benefit or the benefit of a competitor after leaving your company.

13. **Right of first refusal**: This clause in the agreement (also called a "right to match") gives you the right to match offers made by competitors—aimed at stealing away your employee—before your employee quits. This can sometimes take the place of a non-compete agreement, depending on your field and the nature of the work the employee is doing.

14. **Signatures**: the agreement should be signed by the appropriate company representative (such as the CEO) and the employee. See Appendix B for an employment contract example.

Contracts for independent contractors look similar to those for employees in that they should cover the scope of work required, compensation, confidentiality, non-solicitation, and invention assignment.

A note for those operating in California: California employment law is sufficiently different from other states that your employment contract will likely need to be more robust than the outline provided here. A few of the additional requirements on hiring labor in California include reimbursement for business-related expenses, baring non-competes clauses, baring mandatory arbitration, etc. Do some research to make sure your employment contract so you don't violate anything in the state code.

Step 38: Send Out An Employee Handbook

Your company's Employee Handbook is supposed to tell your employees what the company is about, how they fit in, and where to take their questions. It's an important part of employee onboarding. Some good things to include in an employee handbook include the following:

1. Your company's mission statement, vision, and goals.
2. Your company's core values, uniqueness factor, and culture.
3. HR and legal information related to employment (notably, make sure they know who to talk to about questions or issues that arise).
4. Your company's policies about responsiveness, hours worked, communication, and so on (it's okay to reiterate sections from the employment contract).
5. Employee benefits and perks.

For startups, your handbook could be a page or two long. It will certainly need development over time.

Along with the handbook, you might send each new employee an Acknowledgement and Receipt of Employee Handbook notice (you can find templates of these online). By signing, the employee signifies that they received and read through the policies.

For more info on how to develop company culture, I found Conscious Culture (conscious.org) to be helpful. Each company is going to be different, so use Conscious Culture as a starting point and then figure out how to make it your own.

Step 39: Get I-9S Filled Out

The first thing your new employees should do is fill out an I-9 form for verification of identity and eligibility to work in the U.S. You should provide each employee with the form, and he/she should fill it out. You should then review it and make sure the information looks legitimate before proceeding with business.

Once completed, you should keep the I-9s in your company files. You do not have to file them with the state or the Fed, but you must be ready to deliver them to government officials upon request. Blank I-9 forms—and accompanying instructions—can be downloaded from the IRS's website.

Step 40: Get W-4S Filled Out

The second thing your new employees should do is fill out a W-4 form, which tells you (the employer) how much to withhold from their checks for tax purposes. Your employees must complete their W-4s (and their I-9s) before you can pay them.

You do not have to send these forms to the IRS, but you do need to keep them in your records and deduct the proper amount from your employees' paychecks each pay period. You can find blank W-4 forms on the IRS website.

Step 41: Set Up Direct Deposit

Get banking information from your employees and set up direct deposit. Once you add the new accounts, some banks may require a few verification steps that can take a few days (such as sending small sums to and from the other bank). Make sure you've thoroughly verified the account before you send the first paycheck.

Payroll services like Gusto, Rippling, and Trinet are worth looking into for how they simplify the process and do their own account verification, though some banks have their own version of a payroll service. Not only do these services make sure your people get paid, they also generate accounting reports that make your life easier at tax season.

Note that paying employees living in other countries can be difficult because transactions can get rejected. Using a third-party payroll service with a presence in the state or country where your employee works is an easy way to solve the problem. Deel (letsdeel.com) is a fantastic tool for sending international payments.

Compare these companies for their benefit offerings:

1. Rippling (rippling.com)
2. Gusto (gusto.com)
3. Justworks (justworks.com) - For payroll, benefits, HR, and compliance.
4. Guideline
5. Trinet, ADP (trinet.com,) - Similar to the above but not optimized for startups.
6. Savvy (gosavvy.com) - Reimbursements for health insurance which employees get on their own.

Step 42: Set Up Benefits

If you provide your employees with benefits, make sure your new hires get all set up shortly after they start working. This will include their 401k match, insurance, and any other benefits you promised in their employment contracts.

If your company is smaller and isn't ready to provide full-fledged benefits, but you still want to offer something, you can provide monthly stipends to your employees that can be used to reimburse health, dental, or other expenditures. Justworks

(justworks.com) is one option for taking care of payroll, benefits, and compliance all at once.

Step 43: Pay Signing Bonuses

If you've promised any stock options or cash bonuses upon signing, make sure to deliver these timely. Bonuses are taxed as "supplemental income" using the IRS form 1040E and are withheld differently than taxes on salary. With a bonus, the employee will still get the same amount in their pocket when all the dust settles, but it will take longer because bonuses are typically withheld at a higher rate.

Step 44: Systematize Performance Documentation

Almost all states have at-will employment, which means you don't need any specific reason to terminate an employee (as long as it isn't an improper reason). Exceptions to at-will employment include specific policies enacted by the state, such as it being illegal to fire someone for refusing to break the law or for filing a workers' compensation claim.

If you find yourself in a situation where you need to give a reason to fire someone, having documentation of the employee's performance will save you a lot of trouble (and potentially a lawsuit). Consequently, you should find a way to measure employee performance and build a system for recording it, measuring performance against the expectations you established in the employee agreement.

Letting people go aside, you should also give written feedback and document performance because it helps people improve.

There's no one system that will work for everyone, so do what makes sense for your team. You might record monthly stats for key performance indicators, keep records of all complaints made by managers or other team members, etc. Whatever you do, document it in connection to your employees' job descriptions.

And there you have it! Your team is now ready to be led down the adventurous path of a fast-growing startup.

SECURITIES LAW CONSIDERATIONS FOR CRYPTO COMPANIES

Main points:

1. Cryptocurrencies and other digital assets may be considered securities and subject to federal and state securities laws based on the "Howey test."
2. Companies offering securities to the public or through an ICO may need to register with the Securities and Exchange Commission (SEC).
3. There are exemptions from the registration requirements, such as Regulation D for accredited investors and Regulation A for smaller offerings.

Cryptocurrencies and other digital assets are often considered securities, which means they are subject to federal and state securities laws. It's important for founders of crypto companies to be aware of these laws and to ensure compliance in order to avoid legal issues down the line. This chapter will provide an overview of the key securities law considerations for crypto companies in the USA.

Securities laws are a set of laws that regulate the offer and sale of securities, which include stocks, bonds, and other investment instruments. The main purpose of securities laws is to protect investors from fraud and other misconduct, and to ensure that they have access to complete and accurate information when making investment decisions.

Securities laws were formed in response to a number of financial scandals that occurred in the late 19th and early 20th centuries. These scandals led to a loss of public trust in the financial markets and a need for greater regulation.

Securities laws try to prevent fraud and other misconduct by requiring companies to disclose certain information to the public when they are offering or selling securities. This includes information about the company's financial condition, management, and the risks associated with the investment.

In the USA, securities laws are administered by the Securities and Exchange Commission (SEC), which is a federal agency that is responsible for enforcing federal securities laws and regulating the securities industry.

Step 45: Definition Of A Security

The Securities Act of 1933 defines a security as "any note, stock, treasury stock, security future, security-based swap, bond, debenture, evidence of indebtedness, certificate of interest or participation in any profit-sharing agreement, collateral-trust certificate, preorganization certificate or subscription, transferable share, investment contract, voting-trust certificate, certificate of deposit for a security, fractional undivided interest in oil, gas, or other mineral rights, or, in general, any interest or instrument commonly known as a 'security', or any certificate of interest or participation in, temporary or interim certificate for, receipt for, or warrant or right to subscribe to or purchase, any of the foregoing."

This definition is broad and includes many types of digital assets, such as cryptocurrencies, tokens, and other digital securities. The definition has been interpreted by the courts and the Securities and Exchange Commission (SEC) to include digital assets that meet the "Howey test," which looks at whether an investment involves:

1. an investment of money
2. in a common enterprise
3. with the expectation of profits
4. primarily from the efforts of others

If an investment meets all four of these criteria, it is likely to be considered a security and subject to federal and state securities laws.

It's important for founders of crypto companies to be aware of the Howey test and to carefully consider whether their offerings could be considered securities. If you are unsure whether your offering is a security, it's a good idea to consult with an experienced securities attorney.

Step 46: Registration Requirements

If you are offering securities to the public or selling securities through an initial coin offering (ICO), you may be required to register with the Securities and Exchange Commission (SEC). The registration process can be complex and time-consuming, and it's important to work with an experienced securities attorney to ensure that you are in compliance with all relevant laws and regulations.

Step 47: Exemptions From Registration

There are certain exemptions from the registration requirements that may be available to crypto companies, depending on the specifics of the offering and the type of securities being offered. Some common exemptions include:

1. Regulation D: This exemption allows companies to sell securities to accredited investors without registering

the offering with the SEC. Accredited investors are individuals or entities with a high net worth or income, as defined by the SEC.

2. Regulation A+: This exemption allows companies to offer and sell securities to the general public, subject to certain limitations on the amount of money that can be raised.

3. Regulation Crowdfunding: This exemption allows companies to raise money from the general public through crowdfunding platforms, subject to certain limitations on the amount of money that can be raised and the type of securities that can be offered.

It's important to carefully consider which exemption, if any, is most appropriate for your offering and to work with an experienced securities attorney to ensure compliance.

Step 48: State Securities Laws

In addition to federal securities laws, you may also be subject to state securities laws, known as "blue sky" laws. These laws can vary from state to state, and it's important to be aware of and comply with the requirements in any state where you are offering or selling securities.

Step 49: Ongoing Reporting Requirements

If you are required to register your offering with the SEC, you will also be subject to ongoing reporting requirements. This may include filing periodic reports (such as quarterly and annual reports) and disclosing material events (such as changes in ownership or material contracts).

Step 50: Regulation By The Cftc

Even if a token sale is not considered a security and is not regulated by the SEC, it may still be regulated by the Commodity Futures Trading Commission (CFTC) if it involves futures or options contracts based on digital assets, or if it takes place in a spot market (a market for the immediate delivery of digital assets). It's important for crypto companies to be aware of and comply with any relevant CFTC regulations.

Step 51: Safts

SAFTs (Simple Agreement for Future Tokens) are a type of investment contract that allow investors to purchase tokens in a future token sale. SAFTs are typically used in ICOs (initial coin offerings) as a way to raise funds from accredited investors before the tokens are actually created.

SAFTs have been the subject of much debate and scrutiny, as some argue that they are effectively the sale of unregistered securities. The Securities and Exchange Commission (SEC) has stated that some ICOs that use SAFTs may be subject to federal securities laws.

The argument behind the use of SAFTs is that the tokens purchased by investors under a SAFT are "functional tokens". This means that the tokens are not being purchased for the purpose of an investment, but rather as a consumptive product. As a result, the argument goes, these tokens should not be considered securities under the Howey test and should instead be protected only by consumer protection laws.

However, SAFTs have been the subject of much debate and scrutiny, as some argue that they are effectively the sale of unregistered securities. The Securities and Exchange Commission (SEC) has stated that some ICOs that use SAFTs may be subject to federal securities laws, and it has brought enforcement actions against companies that it has determined have violated these laws. In fact, two recent cases already point to tokens promised in SAFTs being classified as securities (SEC v. Kit and SEC v. Telegram). The result has been a decline in the use of SAFTs over the last two years.

It's important for companies to carefully consider whether a SAFT is appropriate for their fundraising efforts and to work with an experienced securities attorney to ensure compliance with all relevant laws and regulations.

Step 52: Token Warrants

A token warrant is a type of investment contract that allows investors to purchase tokens at a later date, often at a discounted price. Token warrants are similar to stock warrants.

Warrants are similar to options, which are securities that give the holder the right (but not the obligation) to buy or sell a specific number of shares of stock at a specific price (the "strike price") on or before a specific date (the "expiration date").

Stock warrants are subject to the same federal and state securities laws as other securities, and they must be registered with the Securities and Exchange Commission (SEC) if they are being offered to the public. It's important for companies to carefully consider whether a stock warrant is appropriate for their fundraising efforts and to work with an experienced securities attorney to ensure compliance with all relevant laws and regulations.

Overall, it's important for founders of crypto companies to be aware of the securities law considerations that may apply to their business and to work with an experienced securities attorney to ensure compliance. This will help to protect investors and avoid legal issues down the line.

ACCOUNTING & TAXES

Main points:

1. After incorporating your company, you will need to pay franchise tax fees and file an annual tax report by March 1st each year.
2. It is important to file taxes on the federal and state levels, including Delaware franchise tax, federal income tax, state income tax, state sales tax, and state franchise tax for any states in which your company conducts business.
3. You may also need to provide VC reports to your investors to track your burn rate and runway.

In this chapter, we will delve into the important topic of taxes and accounting for your business. Let's dive in.

Step 53: Submit An Annual Tax Report And Pay Franchise Tax Fees

You will first need to pay a fee for incorporating in Delaware (or in any other state). These are typically a few hundred dollars, but you can estimate the cost yourself using the state's calculators (corp.delaware.gov/fee/).

You will also need to pay a franchise tax fee and file an annual tax report. These annual payments and reports must be submitted by March 1 each year following incorporation. You can use the state's calculators to figure out what the minimum amount you have to pay is. If you hire a company to take care of it for you, keep in mind that they will tack on a service fee of their own.

Step 54: Invest In An Accounting System

If you have a smaller company, you can fill the accounting role yourself.

You may also want to invest in expense management software like Quickbooks, Xero, or Rydoo that saves you time on bookkeeping tasks and helps you forecast future expenses.

You will feel the consequences of not keeping good records every year at tax time in January.

Taxes aside, accounting prepares you to be audited by the government, investors, potential buyers of your company, and lawyers.

Step 55: Vc Reports

As per your investment contract, you will likely have to make certain reports available to your VCs, so they can track your "burn rate" (how fast you're spending their money versus how fast you're growing). Some VCs might ask you to link your bank account and accounting software to a system like Quaestor, through which they can see exactly how much runway you have left.

Step 56: File Your Taxes

You might receive notices and instructions via mail for completing these when tax time rolls around, but to keep them on your radar, here are the some forms you might have to file:

1. **Delaware franchise tax**. Assuming you are incorporated in Delaware, you'll need to file a Corporate Annual Report by March 1st[t] and pay their franchise tax (a fixed fee of about $300).

2. **Federal income tax**. This is the 21% tax on net company profits you've heard about. You must file federal income tax even if you haven't made any money. You will file this using Form 1120 from the IRS.
3. **State income tax**. You'll need to pay a corporate profit tax in the state you're incorporated in. In Delaware, this happens to be 8.7% (not to be confused with the franchise tax). How much you pay on the state level can also vary based on your product and the types of activities your business engages in.
4. **State sales tax**. This varies between states, but you are typically required to file and pay sales tax quarterly in every state you do significant business in, regardless of whether you had any sales. Events that trigger sales tax being imposed on your company in a given state ("tax nexuses") include having a physical location in the state, having employees working in the state, or reaching a certain sales threshold to residents.
5. **State franchise tax**. Like the franchise tax of the state you incorporated in (i.e. Delaware), you will need to register your corporation and pay a franchise tax with every U.S. state in which your corporation conducts business (measured by a "tax nexus" such as having employees or owning property in a given state). This registration process is often called "foreign qualification" because a corporation is a "foreign" corporation in every state other than the state where it is incorporated.

As you expand your operations, be sure to keep your registration across the U.S. up to date. Note that some states are faster than others. New York typically processes and returns filings in two to three business days, whereas California filing can take up to a month. Various states (notably, California) may also have specific laws that your business must adhere to for hiring, investing, and taxation, and more. Be sure to do your research whenever you do business in a new state.

Paying corporate taxes can be a long and arduous process, so most companies use software from companies like QuickBooks or Xero to help them get it done.

Federal corporate income taxes are due on "the 15th day of the fourth month following the end of the corporation's tax year," according to the IRS. If your fiscal year ends in January, this means April 15. If it ends in June, it means September 30.

If you need a little more time, the IRS will give you a six-month extension if you file Form 7004 by the original deadline. State corporate income taxes are due the same day as your federal income taxes.

Now, because of how corporations are taxed, you'll also need to pay taxes personally on any profits or salary you receive from the business. One of the downsides of having a corporation is this "double taxation" that comes with it. Depending on how you filed your 83(b) election, you can save a lot of money by paying taxes on the estimated value of your shares when you received them, not their current value.

Thankfully, tax software and/or a tax specialist can help you save hundreds of thousands of dollars by alerting you to provisions in the tax code that offer incentives for investors and startups—such as Section 1202, which gives you a tax break on your first $10 million.

PRESS RELEASE

Main Points:

1. A press release is an effective way to get publicity for your new company, particularly if you can leverage connections with your VCs and advisors.
2. It is important to time your press release to coincide with a meaningful event, such as customer acquisition or a new funding round, and target specific writers and publications that are relevant to your industry.
3. To increase the chances of your press release being published, have shareable quotes and images ready, newsjack current events, and keep your release focused on your company's unique selling points. You can also try sending a draft press release as a white paper to reporters or reaching out to industry-specific podcasts and social media influencers.

Although you're technically done incorporating at this point, no company formation is truly complete without a press release.

Step 57: Make Sure Your Website Looks Awesome

You don't need all your pages or full product functionality yet, but make sure the pages you do have are clean, professional, and present your brand in an attractive light. Be sure to test your pages for mobile and tablet friendliness as well. Have a way to capture interested users through a way for them to submit their email, follow you on social media, or join your Discord.

Step 58: Publish A Press Release

A press release is a powerful way to get the word out about your new company. Press releases by already-popular companies are typically picked up automatically by news outlets, but since no one has heard of you yet, you'll have to do some work to get publicity. Now is a great time to leverage your VC's and advisors' connections and see if they can pull any strings.

Time your press release to mean something. Oftentimes, companies will use an announcement to generate interest in either acquiring customers or setting up for the next raise. Time your announcement accordingly

When reaching out to journalists, trying to keep the emails short and snappy and avoid buzzwords that other people are going to be using. Get targeted with the writers you reach out to. Find the person who actually covers what you are building and try to relate what they are interested in covering to what you are doing. Don't email a writer 24 hours before with a pitch. Reporters need time to do interviews, write, and edit.

Look at big publications but also don't overlook smaller publications in your industry. You'd be surprised at the amount of reach targeted papers can actually have and how they can be more targeted at people that are interested in using your product.

Something else that will help you get published is weaving your press release into current events (newsjacking). Speak to industry trends and causes the public cares about at the moment. As a general rule, publish your press release on a Tuesday, Wednesday, or Thursday to capture the most attention—though if you get in with a major news station, just do what they tell you.

Have "shareables" ready: quotes from notable VCs, quotes from customers, an image or media (founder photo, someone using your product photo). A link to a press kit is better than including them in an email.

If that isn't working, rather than waiting, write your own press release and send a draft to reporters as a white-paper article to help get them started. Let them know when it's coming out and ask them to publish it on their platform. The less work they have to do, the more likely they are to get your piece published.

Keep your press release short (about 1 page) and focused on your company's uniqueness factor. Mention your product category and vision for how you'll transform your industry. Describe your core innovation in simple terms anyone can understand. Tell readers who funded you, if you've raised millions and don't mind your competition knowing, mention how much you raised. If you have hardware or a physical product, include an image or it being used.

Reporters aside, industry-relevant podcasts and social media influencers are great ways to tell people about your company. Publish your press release on your website and use that as a home base for your guerilla marketing. Once it's out there, keep pushing to make sure the news spreads.

CONCLUSION

Main points:

1. After completing the process of incorporating your company, it is important to celebrate your accomplishment and congratulate your team, investors, and supporters.
2. Take a moment to reflect on the journey you have been on and the successes that lie ahead for your business.
3. If this book has been helpful to you, consider passing it along to another entrepreneur in need of guidance. If you are a founder seeking additional support or investment, I am available to advise, invest, and help connect you with resources.

Launching a new company is the epitome of a roller-coaster business adventure: terrifying, exhilarating, and breathtaking. Most people never dream of doing it, and of the ones who do put it on their bucket list, even fewer succeed.

...And now you have!

At this point, there's just one more step for you to take.

Step 59: Celebrate

Congratulate yourself, your team, your investors, and the friends and family who supported you along the way.

Together, you've done something big.

I hope you'll take a moment to reflect on how far you've come and the great successes that lie before you.

And if this book has helped you along the way, do a good deed and pass it along to the next entrepreneur you meet.

Step 60: Stay In Touch

As you embark on your entrepreneurial journey, I hope that this book has been a valuable resource for you. If you are a founder and are in need of additional support or investment, I am happy to potentially advise, invest, and help to get other people involved. Please visit
mfischer.xyz/formation to get in touch.

ACKNOWLEDGMENTS

Thank you to those who inspired me along the way and made large contributions toward improving the content of the book:

- Jenn Halweil
- Grace Isford
- Jern Kunpittaya
- Alicia Lew
- Leo Lu
- Ryan McKinney
- Pardis Miri
- Joanna Orlova
- Stash Pomichter
- Alex Poon
- Anna Wang
- Brandon D Wilson

Also special thanks to everyone that read over a copy and helped to edit it:

- Alexander Burns
- Jane Chuprin
- Elise DeCamp
- Milena Fagandini
- Dylan Hunzeker
- Andrej Karpathy
- Kaledora Kiernan-Linn
- Jeremy Li
- Francisco Lopes
- Jay Minga
- Will McTighe

- Cristian Olarasu
- Lorny Pfeifer
- Neel Rai
- Shreenath Regunathan
- Jesse Roth
- Mila Schultz
- Karen Tatarian
- Sarah Tulin
- Caroline Vincent
- Pierce Walker
- Joey Whimple
- Eli Wrightman
- Maria Zlatkova

ABOUT THE AUTHOR

Dr. Michael Fischer

Michael Fischer is the founder of DBDAO.xyz, a database for web3 applications. He lives in NYC where he founded the DeSci NYC group, which hosts monthly meetups on how science can be accelerated using blockchain technologies.

Previously, Michael finished his PhD at Stanford University in computer science where he studied natural language processing and how AI can allow someone to specify a program using natural language. Before, he was an undergrad at Stanford University studying computer science. He is co-author of the book "Regulating AI" and was a teaching assistant at Stanford in the department of computer science and at Stanford Law School for a course taught by a California Supreme Court Justice.

BOOKS BY THIS AUTHOR

Regulating Ai

Until somewhat recently, AI was mostly an academic pursuit that always seemed far away from being released outside of academia. Today, however, AI is touching almost every aspect of human life. As such, there are several emerging legal and policy questions that society will need to reckon with. Although we are faced with new challenges, we have many opportunities to utilize true-and-tested frameworks and legal infrastructure that has been centuries in the making.

This book tries to bring together two disparate fields, law and technology, and give the reader and understanding of their convergence and divergence. We start to answer many of these questions, or at least open the discussion that acknowledges its complexity. This is an exploration of those questions and where possible we try to go over information that might be helpful in appreciating the depth of those questions. As technology and law are two large subjects that span a wide range, we do our best to narrow the scope of the chapters as best we can.

Made in United States
North Haven, CT
13 February 2023

32565890R00055